Wild Cats

Cougars, Bobcats and Lynx

Written by Deborah Hodge

Illustrated by Nancy Gray Ogle

For my children Emily, Mike and Helen - DH
For Lindsay and Connor - NGO

I would like to gratefully acknowledge the review of my manuscript by
Dr. Susan Lumpkin, Director of Communications, Friends of the National Zoo,
and Dr. John Seidensticker, Curator of Mammals, National Zoo, Smithsonian Institute,
both of Washington, D.C.

I would also like to thank Garry J. Grigg, Federal Game Officer, Environment Canada, Canadian
Wildlife Service, for his review of the book and his help in
providing useful suggestions and photocopies.

Special thanks to my editor, Valerie Wyatt, with whom it is a great pleasure to work.

Published in the U.S. by
Kids Can Press Ltd.
85 River Rock Drive, Suite 202
Buffalo, NY 14207

Published in Canada by
Kids Can Press Ltd.
29 Birch Avenue
Toronto, Ontario, Canada M4V 1E2

Edited by Valerie Wyatt
Designed by Marie Bartholomew
Printed in Hong Kong by Wing King Tong
Company Limited

Kids Can Press Ltd. acknowledges with
appreciation the assistance of the Canada Council
and the Ontario Arts Council in the
production of this book.

Canadian Cataloguing in Publication Data

Hodge, Deborah
  Wild cats : cougars, bobcats and lynx

(Kids Can Press wildlife series)
Includes index.
ISBN 1-55074-267-1 (bound)
ISBN 1-55074-357-0 (pbk.)

1. Felidae — Juvenile literature. 2. Pumas —
Juvenile literature. 3. Bobcat — Juvenile
literature. 4. Lynx — Juvenile literature.
I. Ogle, Nancy Gray. II. Title. III. Series.
QL737.C23H63   1995   j599.74'428
C95-931859-3

PA 97 0 9 8 7 6 5 4 3 2 1

Contents

Wild cats

Wild cats are strong, silent hunters. They live in wild places and hide among rocks, trees and bushes. People rarely see them.

Wild cats are mammals. Mammals have furry bodies and they breathe with lungs. They are warm-blooded. Their body temperature stays about the same, even when the outside temperature changes.

Mammal babies are born live.
They drink their mother's milk.

WILD CAT FACT

People sometimes hear wild cats. They make loud screaming noises at mating time.

Kinds of wild cats

There are three kinds of wild cats in North America:
the cougar, the bobcat and the lynx.

Cougars are the biggest and fastest cats in North
America. Adult male cougars weigh about 68 to 73 kg
(150 to 160 pounds). The females are smaller and
weigh 41 to 45 kg (90 to 100 pounds).

Lynx are sometimes called "ghosts of the forest."
Their gray bodies flit through the trees. Adult
lynx weigh from 8 to 11 kg (18 to 25 pounds).

Bobcats are smaller, but they are still twice as big as
a pet cat. They weigh 7 to 10 kg (15 to 22 pounds).
Bobcats have "bobbed" (short) tails.

Where wild cats live

Every wild cat has a habitat – a place where it lives and grows. A habitat provides the food, water, shelter and space the wild cat needs to stay alive.

Cougars roam in mountains and forests, where it is easy to hide and hunt deer. Lynx live in thick forests in the cold north. They stay where they can find snowshoe hares, their favorite food. Bobcats are found in the south, where the weather is warmer.

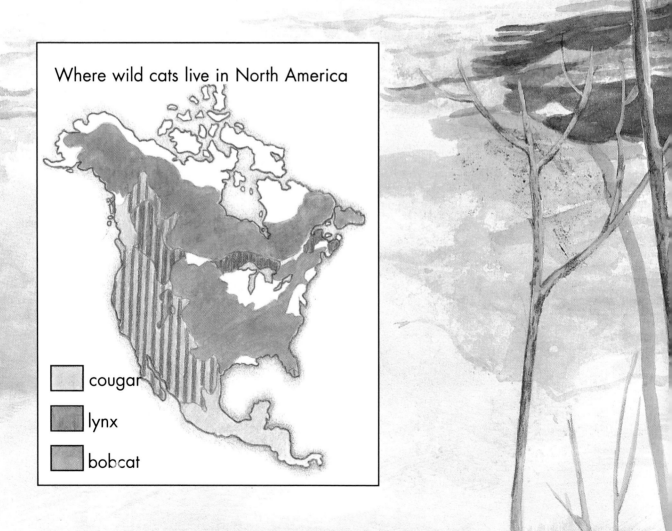

Where wild cats live in North America

cougar

lynx

bobcat

Wild cats live in bushy areas so they can hide from enemies and sneak up on animals they are hunting.

Bobcats need rocks and bushes for hiding.

Wild cat food

Wild cats are meat eaters. They hunt and kill other animals – their prey. They sometimes wait in hunting beds. From these hiding spots, they rest and watch for prey.

Cougars hunt deer. They wait until deer are feeding, early in the morning or just before dark. A cougar hides a deer's body under leaves and dirt and eats it over a few days.

A lynx eats 150 to 200 snowshoe hares a year. When there are few hares, lynx may go hungry and die. Lynx mothers may have fewer babies.

Bobcats hunt animals that are easy to catch. They prefer rabbits and hares, but they also eat other small animals and birds.

How wild cats hunt

Wild cats hunt by day or night. Their special eyes help them see in the dark.

1. Hiding
A lynx hides among the trees.

2. Stalking
On silent paws it stalks its prey – a snowshoe hare.

3. Pouncing

Suddenly, the lynx runs and pounces.
Sharp claws grab the hare.

4. Killing

Strong jaws and pointy teeth make a killing bite. The hare dies quickly. The lynx drags the hare away and eats it in a hidden spot.

Wild cat bodies

The wild cat's body is built for hunting.

Eyes

A wild cat's eyes have large pupils – the middle part of the eye that takes in light. At night, the cat's pupils get very wide and let in more light. This helps the cat see, even in very dim light.

Nose

A wild cat uses its nose to get information. It can even sniff out other wild cat homes.

Teeth and tongue

Sharp teeth can give a killing bite. A prickly tongue pulls meat off bones.

Paws and claws

Razor-sharp claws help the cat catch prey and climb trees. Soft pads on the bottom of the paws let the cat walk silently.

Ears

Keen ears hear prey move.

Fur

Fur keeps the wild cat warm. Its color helps the cat blend in with its surroundings. Fur grows longer in winter.

Bones

A wild cat's bones are light but strong. Its skeleton bends easily for jumping, stretching and twisting. Long back legs help the cat jump.

Muscles

Thick muscles make the wild cat strong.

How wild cats move

Wild cats usually pad along on tiptoes. They crouch down low to follow prey. Wild cats have good balance for leaping and turning. Cougars, lynx and bobcats can swim and climb trees.

A cougar can run very fast, but only for a short distance. Wild cats must catch their prey in three or four long jumps.

A bobcat uses its sharp claws to get up a tree.

Lynx paws work like snowshoes. The toes spread out so the lynx can run on top of the snow.

Wild cat homes

A wild cat lives on a home range – an area of land it claims as its own. Wild cats travel around their home ranges to hunt. They stay close to their prey and sleep wherever there is cover.

When a female wild cat is ready to have babies, she makes a den. In the den, the new kittens are safe from enemies and protected from the weather.

Mother cougars make dens in rock piles and caves. Or they find shelter in deep brush, under fallen logs or tree roots.

A bobcat makes her den between rocks.

A lynx mother makes her den in the thick forest. She nestles under the roots of a fallen tree or inside a hollow log.

How wild cats are born

Kittens are born in a dark, hidden den. Two to four lynx and bobcat kittens are usually born in the spring. Two or three cougar kittens can be born at any time of year.

The new kittens are tiny, blind and almost helpless. They crawl to their mother's nipples and drink her milk. She washes them with her tongue.

A mother will move her kittens to a new den if enemies are near.

Bobcat kittens stay warm and cozy close to their mother's body.

How wild cats grow and learn

Soon the kittens are soft, furry bundles of energy. They wrestle and chase one another. They practice stalking and pouncing.

When the wild kittens are about a month old, their mother brings them meat to eat. At first they only sniff the meat, play with it and chew on the bones. They quickly learn to eat it. Before long the kittens go hunting, too. They copy their mother and learn how to stalk prey.

Wild kittens stay with their mother until they can hunt and protect themselves. Lynx and bobcat kittens usually leave their mother when they are less than a year old. Cougar kittens stay with their mother longer – up to 20 months.

Lynx kittens like to play.

Wild kittens have spotted fur so they can hide among rocks and trees.

How wild cats protect themselves

A wild cat has few enemies. Its big teeth and sharp claws keep most animals away.

Larger animals, such as cougars and wolves, sometimes prey on bobcats and lynx. The cats hide or climb trees to escape.

An angry bobcat flattens its ears, snarls and whips its tail back and forth. It warns other animals to stay away.

Wild cats and people

Wild cats try to live far away from people. But people move into wild areas and disturb the home ranges of wild cats.

People clear forests to build new houses and roads, so the wild animals who live there must move. The deer move to find food, so the cougars must follow. The lynx must follow the snowshoe hare. If there is no place to go, the animals die.

As wild areas get smaller, there are fewer places for wild cats to live.

WILD CAT FACT

Hunters sometimes see cougar tracks behind their own footprints. This tells them that a big cat was following them!

Wild cats need lots of wild space to roam and raise their young.

Wild cats of the world

Here are some of the wild cats that live around the world.

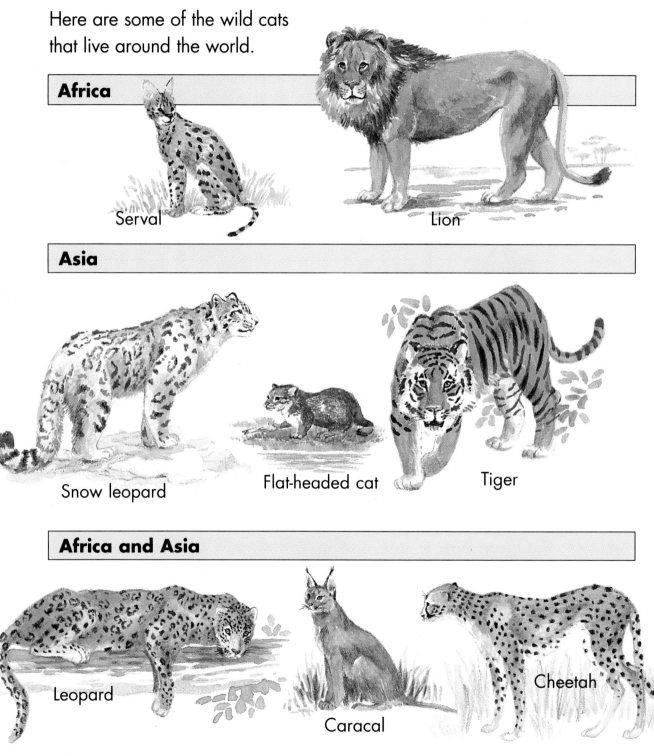

Africa

Serval

Lion

Asia

Snow leopard

Flat-headed cat

Tiger

Africa and Asia

Leopard

Caracal

Cheetah

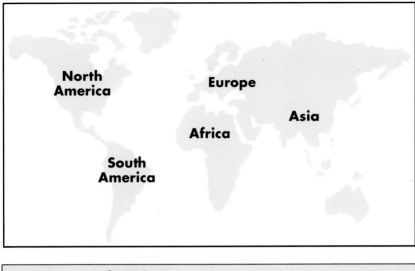

Europe and Asia

Eurasian lynx

South America

Jaguarundi

Jaguar

Ocelot

Wild cat signs

Cougar

Bobcat

Lynx

Tracks

Wild cat tracks look like large cat or dog prints.
The two footprints on the right are the size of a real
cougar's prints. How does your hand size compare?

Scrapes

A wild cat marks out its home range by making
scrapes. It scratches up a small pile of dirt or leaves
and sprays urine on top. The urine leaves a strong
smell. Other cats sniff the scrape and stay away.

Scat

Some wild cats bury their scat (body waste). Others
leave it on top of a scrape. The scat often has pieces
of bone or fur in it.

Words to know

den: a home for a mother wild cat and her kittens

habitat: the place where an animal naturally lives and grows

home range: an area of land that an animal lives on and claims as its own

hunting bed: a hiding spot where a wild cat waits and watches for prey

kitten: young wild cat

mammal: a warm-blooded animal with hair covering, whose babies are born live and fed mother's milk

mating time: a time when a male and female wild cat come together to produce kittens

prey: an animal that is hunted for food

stalk: to follow an animal quietly and carefully in order to catch it

warm-blooded: having a warm body temperature, even when it is cold outside

Index